The Common Summer

Other books by Robert Wallace

This Various World and Other Poems (1957)
Views from a Ferris Wheel (1965)
Ungainly Things (1968)
Critters (1978)
Swimmer in the Rain (1979)
Girlfriends and Wives (1984)

Poems on Poetry (1965)
Writing Poems (1982, 1986)

The Common Summer

New & Selected Poems

Robert Wallace

Carnegie Mellon University Press
Pittsburgh 1989

Acknowledgments

811.54
WAL

New

Acknowledgment is gratefully made to editors of the following in which some of these poems first appeared: *The American Scholar, The Antioch Review, The Atlantic, The Blue Hotel, The Cape Rock, The Christian Science Monitor, Commonweal, Counter/Measures, Epoch, Gamut, Harper's Magazine, Hiram Poetry Review, Jumping Pond, The Kenyon Review, The Laurel Review, Light Year, The New Republic, The New York Times, The New Yorker, North Dakota Quarterly, The Ohio Review, Open Places, Patchwork, Pembroke 19, Phoebe, Poetry, Poetry Northwest, Poetry Now, Poets On:, The Reporter, The Saturday Review, Shenandoah, South Coast Poetry Review, The Southern Poetry Review, The Southern Review, Tar River Poetry, Three Rivers Poetry Journal, The Virginia Quarterly Review.*

"Dog's Song" was originally published as a poster by PLGC, "The Gold Nest" as a broadside by Stuart Wright, "The Author" as a chapbook by Bits Press.

Poems in the first section are from *Poets of Today IV* (Scribner's, 1957), *Views from a Ferris Wheel* (Dutton, 1965), *Ungainly Things* (Dutton, 1968). Those in the second section are from *Swimmer in the Rain* (Carnegie Mellon, 1979), *Girlfriends and Wives* (Carnegie Mellon, 1984), and after.

*   *   *

Publication of this book is supported by grants from the National Endowment for the Arts in Washington, D.C., a Federal agency, and from the Pennsylvania Council on the Arts.

or 10.95/7.49 - 11/89

Library of Congress Catalog Card Number 88–70526
ISBN 0–88748–079–9
ISBN 0–88748–080–2 (Pbk.)

I. Title

Contents

1953 – 1968

1969 – 1987

for Tina

Forgetful of the flood,
in a busy hour all are debarked and gone
down from Ararat. By sunfall the voices
of their going have vanished. The ark alone
centers their outward footprints . . .

and no one knows
what green the unreturning raven found.

Ungainly Things
1953 – 1968

"For a long time I'd had in my mind the memory of a Chinese dog I'd seen somewhere. And then one day I was walking along the rue de Vanves in the rain, close to the walls of the buildings, with my head down, feeling a little sad, perhaps, and I felt like a dog just then. So I made that sculpture. But it's not really a likeness at all. Only the sad muzzle is anything of a likeness. Anyway, people themselves are the only real likenesses. I never get tired of looking at them. When I go to the Louvre, if I look at the people instead of at the paintings or sculptures, then I can't look at the works of art at all and I have to leave."

— Alberto Giacometti

Adagio

Old kings of China riding
on golden plumed white asses,
that toil up, slightly nodding,
through rocky mountain-passes,
in the bright and glass-blue weather,
old kings of China riding
in a white and golden line.

Up past the berry bushes
and the white-bark elms they go,
beyond the rivers' splashes,
and the summits' glistering snow,
in the bright and glass-blue weather,
old kings of China riding
in a white and golden line.

They go riding, riding, high
in an endless slow procession
from the mountains through the sky,
riding slowly to the sun,
in the bright and glass-blue weather,
old kings of China riding
in a white and golden line.

The Garden Snail

This backyard cousin to the octopus
sees through two filmy stems

on his head, at need can peer round
corners, and so betrays his huge

timidity. He moves on his single
elastic foot seldom, preferring

anonymity to danger, seems
often to be meditating a very tough

problem, likes green leaves and water.
Shyness is his prime virtue,

though I have seen one, on a blue day
in summer, go climbing all afternoon

with his brown shell up the wobbly tall grass,
for a good look-round at the wide world.

The Storm

Noonlight is sudden-full of the spirits
of dead butterflies, moving
— like a holiday!
surely, all that have ever been!
They are like flowers in the bushy pine,
on hedges, trees; fluttering
knee-deep in the fields; flailing
out of a sky thick with them as if with snow.
I go up on the roof to see them.
The landscape is a blizzard of hues,
farms going under,
— wingbeats, petals, flakes —
they come in at my lips and eyelids,
they fly in the currents of my blood;
friendly, they kill with such gentle wings,
knives stroking as softly as eyelashes.
The day hums in their overshadowings
— they will cover the electric lines;
even the mountains will be buried
in this colored Pompeii,
in these deep, bright ashes.

The Noise That Woke Me Strangely

was my neighbor chopping wood at midnight.
The floodlight, from his porch, made him a shadow
dancing over a larger shadow dancing
crazily about him, arms and all angles
where the house cornered into shrubby dark.
He laid on stroke, and stroke, and stroke. The grass
of summer shone a fiercer, April green
in the light's ellipse; the ax, about his head
darted like a bird startled from its sleep,
and couldn't leave the light alone.

What put his hands like prayer on the ax handle,
later he never said. But by morning
whatever it was had split enough good oak
to burn it voicelessly into the winter nights —
smoke, drifting to the faraway stars. Whenever
it was, no one was watching when he stopped.

As always, in the morning, he waved cheerily
from his leafed garden as I drove, waving, past.

The Two Old Gentlemen

Though the house had burned years ago,
with everything in it,
all that had been brought out in the wagons,
all that had been added since,
the photographs, the pink-flowered paper,
the stuffed furniture from St. Louis,
the blue gilt set of Dickens their father
had ordered from the salesman out from St. Louis —

Though the house had burned years ago,
they always talked of it
and of the times there had been in it
when they were boys, before they were boys,
the uncle who had been wounded at Antietam
and had come west and died before they were born,
their mother churning on the porch, the arrowheads
they once found along the banks of the green creek —

Though the house had burned years ago,
with everything in it,
they sat talking, these childless gentlemen,
in the sun-high field where the hay was making,
these gentle children by the big red baler,
talking of Mr. Micawber and Little Nell,
of Dombey, and Krook who turned to smoke,
and Pickwick travelling the road to Norwich.

Total

Crossing Ohio, all of a July afternoon,
the turnpike
in sunlight before us, behind us,
we hit on 27 butterflies,
crushing against windshield and shiny steel.
White. Brown. Orange. Looping
easily out of the woods, off of the fields,
swallowtails, monarchs, lemon-wings, glass-wings, white
     cabbages.

Twenty-seven!

               East of Elyria,
one mottled wing
hung flapping to the glass terribly
before hurtling loose and
overhead;
mostly, however, they left colored stars,
nova-stains, against our racing sky.

The Star-Nosed Mole

Once neighbor to the dinosaur,
    dweller
        in the underground,

denizen of these old lands,
    swimmer
        in the earth, his element,

the star-nosed mole
    favors
        our fields and farms,

browses beneath the happy suburbs,
    sightless
        where the bright years pass

above him.
    Fierce
        in love and battle, little,

ungainly with his hidden ears,
    he forages
        the deep, rich country

of the dark. On his snout he bears
    before him,
        always, a naked fringe

of fleshy feelers, rose-colored,
    a star;
        a pugnacious flower of darkness,

travelling the hungry tunnels
    scooped
        by powerful claws,

active in all seasons,
    moving,
        at all hours searching

eyelessly for his endless dinner,
    star tentacles
        in constant motion —

lowly
    Arcturus,
        whose hunger is his twinkle.

Sometimes you will see him,
    in winter,
        glossy, come a moment

out into the open sunlight,
    stand
        in all the brilliance he can see,

in the wind, and vanish
    again
        into his darkling courses.

A Snapshot for Miss Bricka Who Lost in the
Semifinal Round of the Pennsylvania Lawn
Tennis Tournament at Haverford, July, 1960

Applause flutters onto the open air
like starlings bursting from a frightened elm,
and swings away across the lawns
in the sun's green continuous calm

of far July. Coming off the court,
you drop your racket by the judge's tower
and towel your face, alone, looking off,
while someone whispers to the giggling winner,

and the crowd rustles, awning'd in tiers
or under umbrellas. Bluely, loss
hurts in your eyes — not loss merely,
but seeing how everything is less

that seemed so much, how life moves on
past either defeat or victory,
how, too old to cry, you shall find steps
to turn away. Now others rally

behind you in the steady glare;
the crowd waits in its lazy revel,
holding whiskey sours, talking, pointing,
whose lives (like yours) will not unravel

to a backhand, a poem, or a sunrise,
though they may wish for it. The sun
brandishes softly his swords of light
on faces, grass, and sky. You'll win

hereafter, other days, when time
is kinder than this worn July
that keeps you like a snapshot: losing,
once, made you completely beautiful.

The Double Play

In his sea-lit
distance, the pitcher winding
like a clock about to chime comes down with

the ball, hit
sharply, under the artificial
banks of arc lights, bounds like a vanishing string

over the green
to the shortstop magically
scoops to his right whirling above his invisible

shadows
in the dust redirects
its flight to the running poised second baseman

pirouettes
leaping, above the slide, to throw
from mid-air, across the colored tightened interval,

to the leaning-
out first baseman ends the dance
drawing it disappearing into his long brown glove

stretches. What
is too swift for deception
is final, lost, among the loosened figures

jogging off the field
(the pitcher walks), casual
in the space where the poem has happened.

After the Swimmer

Clear, the shaken water
busies in its claws
clouds, light,
from which he climbed.

In the Field Forever

Sun's a roaring dandelion, hour by hour.
Sometimes the moon's a scythe, sometimes a silver flower.
But the stars! all night long the stars are clover,
Over, and over, and over!

from THE DICTIONARY ZOO

The Walrus

Looking like 1905,
though considerably older,
obviously longing to wive
and sport where the air is apt to be colder

than here, the walrus sits
between Walpurgis Night and waltz,
nicely suspended between the flesh's and the spirit's
comfortable faults,

but ignoring both, looking straight ahead,
a dreamy lounger in the Arctic sun,
fin-feet spread,
exile from the blizzard coasts where ice floes run;

($\frac{1}{120}$) natural size,
the leathery whale-horse (from the Dutch),
by the look in his heavy-lidded eyes,
doesn't like it much.

The Brontosaurus

Thunder-lizard (Greek) and huge as you want, he's
    really
        well-meaning
           and kind —
though clumsy, a nibbler of grass and of leaves,
    with a tiny,
        prehistoric
           mind.

Next door neighbor here and now to the Brontës,
    Emily
        and Charlotte
        and Anne,
the slow-witted brontosaurus behaves
    as well
        as he possibly
        can.

The Gerrymander

This long-necked, mean old political buzzard
— whose note was heard

first in Massachusetts by Governor Gerry —
has a beak of Salisbury,

rump of Lynn, and claws of Salem and Marblehead,
and wings (now flag-drooping) whose spread

can overshadow the state,
a modern political equivalent for Fate.

Now, here, reduced in size,
he has fixed his eyes

across the page on *get, get ahead, get around, get at.*
Skinny, he wants to get fat.

Like the American eagle, a bird of prey,
he doesn't like not to have his way.

The Jaguar

On the right-hand page, this jaguar
that's
not a car

has turned his back
on
a jackal and a rabbit (jack)

(both quite scary-solemn)
in
the left-hand page's left-hand column.

The doe-eared jackal looks up,
and
the hare is ready to hop.

Clearly, plainly,
it
isn't their knowing merely, mainly,

that he'll eat them if he can
(being,
after all, no vegetarian)

that makes them so very, very glum,
but
that they'll have to come —

as the pages close —
right
under his nose!

To a Bird Watcher, But Gratefully

for R. L.

They are Arctic terns I watched all summer,
you tell me
: flat-black-capped, with pointy wings,
above the salt marsh or like a plummet dropping
into the inlet and emerging
from the splash, swimming into the air,
a minnow crosswise in the beak.

The crested fellow on the piling
is a kingfisher.

The white ones in the marsh are egrets,
not herons,
in the twisty wind-row cedars.

That much for sure, though the sandpipers
that rolled in a row
before a wave up the beach might have been
Baird's or White-rumped, or some other,
for all of Roger Tory Peterson.

                          Anyway,
it is good to be less ignorant
of their names than I was, or than they are.

Parable for Governors

In 1520
the Italians,
in a formal court,
tried the field mice around Stelvio
on charges of gravely damaging
the crops.

Despite
a spirited
defense, they were condemned
in absentia, and ordered to leave
the countryside "within two weeks,"
although

the old,
infirm, or very
young mice were (out of pity)
given twice as long. Farmers were urged
to bridge their creeks
for the exodus —

thus,
in the archives
of the Court of Glorenza
in Val Venosta, near Bolzano, the 2d of May;
where it is not told, however,
whether they left.

A Sight of the Negro Funeral

Leading, the hearse shrugged up onto the highway,
and shinnied off two hundred yards below
— where a little road accepted the way a woods
had curved, and strung its fence and begun to go

staggering up the long hill. Traffic swished by,
hard, and didn't let the small procession out,
its headlights shining in the stormy gloom
like animal eyes. The cars watched, dim, in doubt,

but one by one they turned, and turned off, and joined
the waiting hearse, smoking, beneath the oaks.
And then they started on. Their small dusts, rising,
the red lights pushing on and off, bespoke

the column, dipping, along the ruts and holes
toward what we could not see: the pine-roofed top
of a gray hill, the dismounted mourners halting
beside the long-grassed grave, the earth heaped up,

and all the singing. Four cars like a kite's tail
behind the hearse, old Chevies and a Ford,
they fluttered up where the land rose out of view,
carrying their flowery cargo toward their Lord.

Closing Down

Through rinsing the car for the last time
before winter, I broke up the hose
and coiled its sections, stiff with summer,
and carried them one by one through
the three-foot-high plank door leading
under one corner of the house, into
a shallow dirt-floored place of boards
old buckets bicycle wheels poles shingles,
piled and cluttered. The light followed
me in. Through the door the world
was like a sullen photograph
I climbed back into, going out;
the crab grass, lacking its one last mowing,
seemed a junkyard of ruined antennae
below the sagging pear tree's fountain,
to the crawling eye. I hung the hoses
from back-wall hooks. On the final trip,
I came with pliers to reach among
the ghostly cobwebs and shut off
the pipe that runs along the rafters
to outside, and open the copper cock
that lets the water guzzle from the pipe.
I had gone, hunched like a queer spider,
in and out the tiny door; when I stood
again, at last, upright in the air,
the painty hook forced in on darkness,
I was surprised I had not closed
October down. The pine rose still
green-fired in the tall sky, the gold fields
rode still moored in the lines of light
like a fleet rocking with all arrivals.
I stood, among my sponges and bucket,
amazed, like a tiny Gulliver,
at how huge and shining the broad world was.

Among the Finger Lakes

These great brown hills move in herds, humped like bison,
before the travelling eye. Massive above the farms, they file
and hulk daylong across every distance; and bending come
as the sun sinks (orange and small) beyond their heavy
    shoulders,
shaggy at evening, to drink among the shadowy lakes.

Omen

The big crows always come
before rain,
three of them; in the sunny pine,
or on the fence, among roses; somewhere.

We do not see them,
except then.
So far they have foretold
only the rain

with their cawings
— muddy fields
and the closed windows
at evening.

A Last Photograph

Less love than that no one else can care
joins them — now, in pre-dawn kitchen light,
a cup of spoons for iron flowers —
to that slimmer, smiling, earlier pair
who posed outside the oak church door
or held the gleaming ship's rail tight.

Hereafter strangers, they attend
the hour that keeps them, like story lovers
unable to go beyond *THE END*,
like Pip and Estella in their street,
who must unhappily meet
in the only scene now they'll have forever.

Manifesto for a Little Brass Key

I found it
once in deep grass where it shone

from the vertical shadows, brushing it
free of leaf-stuff, grass bits,

the colors of the sun —
tiny, tuneful, for locking and unlocking nothing,

ringing it among all the practical keys
of my life

that let me enter the places I am known
— look, who am I to say

there isn't a door it was meant for
opening, into love

or money or some other good thing:
and I'll go through.

What He Says

Raspberries splash, redly
   in their leaves;
      squirrels

squabble in the pine-tops.
   An old man,
      wearing

a sweater in warm July,
   breathes
      the same morning as the birds,

goes, talking among flowers
   beautiful as he is,
      bending,

leaves at his elbow.
   What he says,
      by himself, wandering

in the sunny garden,
   need not be true,
      nor useful.

In a Spring Still Not Written Of

This morning
with a class of girls outdoors, I saw
how frail poems are
in a world burning up with flowers,
in which, overhead,
the great elms
— green, and tall —
stood carrying leaves in their arms.

The girls listened equally
to my drone, reading, and to the bees'
richocheting
among them for the blossom on the bone,
or gazed off at a distant mower's
astronomies of green
and clover, flashing,
threshing in the new, untarnished sunlight.

And all the while, dwindling,
tinier, the voices — Yeats, Marvell, Donne —
sank drowning
in a spring still not written of,
as only the sky
clear above the brick bell-tower
— blue, and white —
was shifting toward the hour.

Calm, indifferent, cross-legged
or on elbows half-lying in the grass —
how should the great dead
tell them of dying?
They may come to time for poems at last,
when they have found they are no more
the beautiful and young
all poems are for.

Giacometti's Dog

lopes in bronze:
    scruffy,
        thin. In

the Museum of Modern Art
    head
        down, neck long as sadness

lowering to hanging ears
    (he's eyeless)
        that hear

nothing, and the sausage
    muzzle
        that leads him as

surely as eyes:
    he might
        be

dead, dried webs or clots of flesh
    and fur
        on the thin, long bones — but

isn't, obviously,
    is obviously
        traveling intent on his

own aim: legs
    lofting
        with a gaiety the dead aren't known

for. Going
    onward in one place,
        he doesn't so much ignore

as not recognize
    the well-
        dressed Sunday hun-

dreds who passing, pausing make
    his bronze
        road

move. Why
    do they come to admire
        him,

who wouldn't care for real dogs
    less raggy
        than he

is? It's his tragic
    insouciance
        bugs them? or is

it that art can make us
    cherish
        anything — this command

of shaping and abutting space —
    that makes us love
        even mutts,

even the world, having
    rocks
        and the wind for comrades?

It's not this starved hound,
    but Giacometti's seeing
        him we see.

We'll stand in line all day
    to see one man
        love anything enough.

Ungainly Things

A regular country toad — pebbly,
    squat,
        shadow-green

as the shade of the spruces
    in the garden
        he came from — rode

to Paris in a hatbox
    to Lautrec's
        studio (skylights

on the skies of Paris)
    and stared
        from searchlight eyes,

dim yellow; bow-armed,
    ate
        cutworms from a box,

hopped
    occasionally
        among the furniture and easels,

while the clumsy little painter
    studied
        him in charcoal

until he was beautiful.
    One day
        he found his way

down stairs toward the world
    again,
        into the streets of Montmartre,

and, missing him, the painter-dwarf
   followed,
        peering among cobbles,

laughed at, searching
   until long past dark
        the length of the Avenue Frochot,

over and over,
   for the fisted, marble-eyed
        fellow

no one would ever see again
   except
        in sketches that make ungainly things beautiful.

Fable

The poets stopped. One dawn or another none of them
wrote anymore;
afterwards, it seemed to have been that simple.

They couldn't explain. Months passed or maybe years, slow
rumors spread;
someone thought they might have stopped forever.

Critics, the last of all to notice, complained.
A Senator spoke
for the record. Letters to the Editor followed, forums,

handsome offers. The President urged resumption of "this
magnificent
public service." The Dow-Jones slid a fraction.

But they were gone, as down in darkling green
crabs sink sideways
past light, or as a butterfly closes his wings

upon a fence wire in the frostiness of October.
No one who could say
truly what such a loss might mean came forward.

Nothing in fact seemed to change. Days still were days;
moon, stars went along
shining as before. Lovers loved. Heroes had wars.

The small birds vanished and returned, sang;
schoolyards lay dusty
in August sun. The world went on in smoking rains,

in red and glass-gold weathers, in snowy mornings
when the butterflies
were dead and sticks walked upright on the rivers.

Out for Stars

We walked out late, leaning back for stars
beneath the staked-down tent of dark,
gawking there like foreigners
at high, and myriad, and stark,

until we turned tired from them, stiff-
eyed with staying for a meteor's track,
and saw below, in the tide-creek's slough,
faint bits of glassy fire in the black

that flowed around the pilings: glowed,
and faded, and glowed again. Deep in,
haze-firefly green; and where it rode
the crinkling surface, pale blue winks

and sparks. A long-handled net we swished
them with, they made burn all blue-white
as if electrified. We fished
some up — clear jelly in a match-light,

but in the dark striped, icy fire
the net strained out, let slide through, plop
and glowing back into the choir.
Soft stars! that let us take them up.

Between Equals

A dragonfly blue as the June Atlantic
slim as its horizon
came over the dunes:

helicoptering off and on
a grass beside my chair.

A small event.
He stayed. And went.

Fly in December

In an old, dark house —
where the thick light held us
bowled in glass —

looping from nowhere, furious, he came
flinging, bitter,
rude, a drunken aim

zanging, unzipping halves of the air
all afternoon and evening,
singing black in eye and ear

or, overhead, rode invisibly
in the terrier's shouldered, worried glance
on some vague journey

through doors into other rooms,
back, wrestling
whatever his angel or doom:

the sweetness gone, the loss of summer.
At midnight, he stopped
suddenly, letting the windows remember

the late snow flying to and fro
again, falling.
Vile, knot that won't pull loose to dying,

is he perched, dumb,
watching in a hundred eyes or — blind? —
having let it come?

Whatever.

    In the old, dark house
we have settled down for the night,
somehow, the three of us.

Taking Back

The brave little roses I got you Saturday, coming
from the dentist's in the rain
— pink, and gay soft white
in green tissue —

shed petals now which singly
drop, and drift like a circle of swans
heedless in the pooling light
of the table's top.

Oh, I take them back,
in the barren weather I take them
out, crush them deep in the trash,
hoping you won't notice forever.

Moving

Bookshelves empty, tables lampless, walls
bare, the house is a rubble of moving —
foothills of boxes, trunks
under clouds of ceiling.

                    Friends
said good-bye hours ago, when June twilight
hung on the hills. Now, in dark too
muggy for stars, moths whir to the yellow porch-light,
ping screens. By the one dim floor lamp
among the shadowy undoings of my life,
in a limbo between having gone and having gone,
I sit like a caretaker of my doom.
Not an ashtray or a spoon.
In the real dawn, I will be going.

My friends, sleeping, turned toward
tomorrows without me, will still be dreaming
when I begin to drive the familiar streets and roads
into which the movers will come after me,
in which the flowering sun will come only after me.
If I called anyone now, in this steep hollow
past midnight, all I said would
be from the future.

The phone has been disconnected.

The Common Summer
1969 – 1987

". . . the natural tower of all the world,
The point of survey, green's green apogee."

— Wallace Stevens

In One Place

                    — something
holds up two or three leaves
the first year,

                    and climbs
and branches, summer
by summer,

                    till birds
in it don't remember
it wasn't there.

Dog's Song

Ants look up as I trot by
and see me passing through the sky.

Tulip

It digs the air with green blades,
scooping, curled,
then thrusts out colored gear
in the upper-world

to tap sun and bees and suck
such fuels down
as run its dark machinery
without sound.

The Secret Beyond the Ridge

The pines push upward
each on one leg,
as in a child's drawing.

Even peering, leaning,
only a few
reach the top of the ridge.

The rest press
up behind the leaders,
a green crowd.

Evenings
there is a lot of sighing
among them —

whether because they know
the secret,
or still don't know.

God's Wonderful Drowning Machine

praia de Guincho

From taxis up on the coast road
eight nuns come down the beach
to see God's wonderful drowning machine.

It sparkles, and is very blue.

Pleasure makes a small disorder
among them, laughing, pointing,
at the very edge of the roar.

Out far, a ship slides up and down.

Then in the dazzling sun they go,
shoes clappering their black bells,
back up to the road and sky.

Gear and wheel, belt, pulley, wave.

Swimmer in the Rain

No one but him
seeing the rain
start — a fine scrim
far down the bay,
smoking, advancing
between two grays
till the salt-grass rustles
and the creek's mirror
in which he stands
to his neck, like clothing
cold, green, supple,
begins to ripple.

The drops bounce up,
little fountains
all around him,
swift, momentary —
every drop tossed back
in air atop
its tiny column —
glass balls balancing
upon glass nipples,
lace of dimples,
a stubble of silver
stars, eye-level,
incessant, wild.

White, dripping, tall,
ignoring the rain,
an egret fishes
in the creek's margin,
dips to the minnows'
sky, under which,
undisturbed, steady

as faith the tide pulls.
Mussels hang
like grapes on a piling.
Wet is wet.

The swimmer settles
to the hissing din —
a glass bombardment,
parade of diamonds,
blinks, jacks of light,
wee Brancusi's, chromes
like grease-beads sizzling,
myriad — and swims
slowly, elegantly,
climbing tide's ladder
hand over hand
toward the distant bay.

Hair and eye-brows
streaming, sleek crystal
scarving his throat —
no one but him.

Sea Turtles

By the end of June
tides bring them up the bay,
on into the channels
that wind through the marsh,
riding the flood,
the females — snouts like sticks,
watchful, ready to submerge.

Like stones with wings
they swim, coasting the shallows,
then lumber
out of wet and mud,
up the sand, above the tide-line,
through reeds or bayberry,
crossing roads if need be, climbing,
clacking and hissing at dogs,
not to be deflected.

And they dig with slow
scoops of their leathery back pads,
left, painfully, then right,
bottle-shaped holes in the sand,
and lay their eggs,
which finally, dusty and deliberate,
dancing heavily,
they cover with angel strokes.

You'll see them
again on the out-going tides,
borne on the pouring emerald,
queens,
lonely, buoyant, clear-eyed,
having done
all the seasons require.

Solid and Plain

At dusk, two egrets
like snow
fish the edge of the marsh creek.

One each of everything
that is,
no more; and nothing a symbol

for anything else. Stilt
legs slide
indolently in the water.

Death is pure white, and hunger
takes long
lovely steps, wading into darkness.

August: Decline and Fall

Early, in lemon sun
the pastel houses sweeten the far shore
like laundry.

A music of sparrows on the clear air
sounds and resounds,
and a mud-hen click-clicks in the marsh.

Big as wedding cakes,
two white launches between water and sky
march down the bay.

Residents are out or coming out
onto their docks,
eyes filling with the expensive morning.

Even after the Empire
collapsed, the beautiful weather went on
for years and years.

from GIRLFRIENDS AND WIVES

Melinda Lou

Six, in ringlet curls,
on Normal Street,
your last name the same
as my maternal
grandmother's maiden name,
you biked, played hide-
and-seek and kick-the-can,
played guns, played nurse
with me and Homer Ice,
gave me the bigger
punch-out Valentine,
and moved to Kansas.

The houses are still there
on Normal Street,
smaller by forty years,
and shabbier —
white bungalow, steep terrace
good for sledding,
where you lived. And you
are, once a decade
when I look, small, sweet
and golden in
the locket of my heart,
dead, or in Kansas.

Irene

Gerald went with you before I did,
and teased me about how far you went
with him. He's been dead for twenty years.

Holding your hand in hallways or under a blanket
at football games, sometimes I wondered
how you could ever come to look like your mother.

Across the street from the lights of your house,
winter and summer, we parked and necked and talked.
I forget now why we stopped going steady.

Eyes pale as air, under leafy streetlamps
you let my hand slip down into your blouse
to touch the warm mice soft in their nests.

Ruby

A fierce, hard, pretty body,
a fierce, hard, pretty face:
the high school whore, rank Helen
from the crummy half of town —
have I loved you all my life?

The stories were not true;
you were, perhaps, like us.
The once, petrified with lust,
I asked you out, we hardly
spoke, and did not touch.

Still, if the tales weren't true,
we needed to believe them.
Eyes crinkling with wickedness,
in worn blue jeans your hard ass
was wisdom I learned by heart.

Edith (I)

The girl who came
    out on
        the plank porch of

a farmhouse, set
    on the rough rise
        of hillside from

the little creek where
    your brother
        and I later shot

copperheads curling
    on a branch
        in the slowly tumbling water —

that girl, in shorts
    and curlers,
        sexy, embarrassed,

the brightest
    pupil in her country
        high school, pretty

and Baptist, in a midsummer,
    midweek,
        midafternoon sunlight —

was you,
    for a decade
        as much

myself as I was,
    steady, then lover,
        then wife. As

kids did in those
     years, struggling —
          in countless blue of

the moon and starlit
     and dark nights
          parked by country roads,

the ground fog
     rising and moving
          in dips and fields,

drifting in weeds
     and cornflowers
          colorless as the light —

with buttons,
     zippers, hook-and-eyes,
          elastic, as

complex as Balkan
     politics.
          That girl,

you, with whom
     I laughed and swam,
          played tennis, planned

all the rest of our
     lives — to whom
          through five college-

years away I wrote maybe
     a million words,
          and who,

dearest enemy,
    one year,
        one night, blanket

on the cobwebby, dewy lawn
    behind an empty
        house, woods

around, became
    my first lover, as I
        yours — that

girl, nipples like raspberries,
    back
        arched to the stars.

Bunny

Hair a blond fire, pale as flames,
you lit dim rooms
kindling the damp straw of English November.

There was a man, somewhere, you rarely spoke of
and still were seeing.
But he didn't keep you from seeing me

or, because I wanted to, spending long nights
chatting and fucking
by a gas fire. In March we went to Paris.

That summer, after I was married,
you stopped by on your Vespa,
with windy hair, to say good-bye forever.

You talked a lot about having kiddie-winks —
and are by now, I trust,
the sexiest grandmother in all of Cheshire.

On a flattened Four-Square pack you'd jot,
"I'm free at six if you are.
Luv." You never asked for anything.

Edith (II)

1
And so, in that
    early summer
        of our lives, in

June, cornfields in
    evening sun,
        we became then, suddenly,

young husband and young wife —
    roasting
        chestnuts in the flat

at 55 Eltisley Avenue
    (a year
        later, when we had

gone, Plath and Hughes,
    newly-wed
        too, lived there),

or cycling over
    the cold Moor of Rannoch
        or, later,

canoeing with
    wine and sandwiches
        on the meadow-

banked Brandywine —
    seven years!
        that ended

under stars, in a weedy
    little railroad
        yard in Virginia

where, near
dawn, you boarded
a cloudy-, green-

windowed train
on a journey from which
you never returned.

2
How had we grown
half-strangers, love
flaking

and chipping away?
Did you
insist on running late?

and did I care? It seems,
now,
that my unfaithfulness

poisoned
both of us.
If so, it was a fine,

slow dust, inhaled,
as much
innocence as lust —

Bunny, and then Candy,
each easily
as foolish and young

as we. And knowingly
I let you
make love with Colin

that night after the
     nude swimming
          in the ritzy pool,

while I humped Lucinda
     in the dining
          room, both of them

ten years older, trapping
     us in
          what we wanted. You

were unfaithful, too,
     the last fall,
          alone, in Rome,

although I never asked.
     Minutes,
          small, bored tickings

in the years of our lives —
     "in the way
          a man and woman

in the modern world
     often are,"
          as Williams said —

at the end,
     shrieking, each
          alone.

3
Love fails.
     It is
          as natural

as the failing of the leaves.
    The mystery
        is

going on when love has failed.
    The going on
        is love.

4
Old friend,
    we are no
        longer, as we were,

young and beautiful.
    As when, in that October
        sunlight,

in our new, blue Anglia,
    with the dog —
        old Cedric,

who was then only
    a bright,
        young gentleman-dog —

leaning out the window
    behind us,
        we drove through the yellow

swirls of maple leaves
    and out
        the country roads, past

fields of caved-in corn,
    bounding over
        bridges to the shiny,

musical noises
    of our horn, past
        barns and trees and

people on porches looking up
    until we
        disappeared

up some little hill
    into the sky
        and over and out of sight, waving,

Good-bye, good-bye.
    Above your windbreaker,
        your long neck,

your smile —
    how beautiful you were!
        Did we make love,

later,
    when the sun slanted
        and glittered

out past the empty trees?
    Old friend,
        I would change nothing.

Candace

Circe as Bryn Mawr junior,
daughter of Sol and California,
blond, with an old poet's surname,
you were dangerous enough
to my academic Odysseus,
on one-year contracts and
unused to unasked for love.
The island was Manhattan
to which we fled and where,
in an apartment you borrowed
on the Upper East Side,
we made hurried and not very
satisfactory love. Was it
exams we rushed back for?
Summer, at any rate, was the green
sea that swept between us —
or perhaps embarrassment.
Adultery takes more aplomb,
and more cash, than I had
in those days. A little later,
when I looked you up, you had
a husband and a string of children
in Newton, Massachusetts.
And later still, I saw you had
co-authored a budget TV movie
called "Battered Wives" — come
round at last to Penelope's side.

Dusty

A big, tough, tow-headed Russian Baptist,
with the distrust of men
that invariably makes them say

or do whatever is untrustworthy,
like lying about loving you
or meeting a violent defense with violence,

you fought eagerly night after night
on the musty boathouse couch
long after it was clear your lower-middle-class

virtue wasn't what I admired you for.
Your sopping, silken crotch
was armor, hot and wet, to be stroked

but not got past. Like an oily machine,
it longed to make babies
and turn you frowzy in a flowered cotton dress.

Vicki

Blond and slinky, in the men's shop,
you sold me a knitted tie,
fucked in the car after dinner
like a lean, scratchy kitten
in a tangle of clothes and levers,
and took me home to meet your mother
who was blond and slinky,
about my age. What for I don't
know, but you paid her back.
The white poodle growled at me.

Love Poem Nine Years Later

Not Christmas this time, but
just after. Dirty snow
stripping from a dirty city
like weasels vanishing.

The sunlight runs, lemon,
watery. And you are gone,
a mile maybe, hiding
among your friends, considering

a life of your own.
Across the street a fireplug
in a boy's red knit hat
eyes our house.

The traffic moves, or doesn't.
The year runs down.
There is no sparing one another —
love survives

its failing. Dusk
brings a sparrow or two
into the trees, like leaves
until there are leaves.

Another Self

We keep trying to find each other
but the landscape changes, you're

three-quarters up and the cliff face
crumbles, or the trees keep moving

between us, the woods become water
and I have to turn away and swim

out to the surface. The girl I'm touching
in this strange room wears your face,

we get nearer, you're one of the paratroopers
floating away from the plane. At the last

moment you see me in the window, but
it's snowing. You've never been to Paris.

In the First Place

Go on living. The big moon,
a night or so off full, shines
in. It makes a square of light
like white powder on the floor —
bonelight, scoured of its red meat.
It is the sun, reflected.
And on the ceiling of the room,

another square of this light,
dimmer, twice reflected now,
by moon and by the salt creek
runneling below the window,
glimmers. A moving surface
of wave-shadows, dark ripples
like flights of misty, vague birds

passing, passing. Both moon shapes,
which are trapezoids really,
move east, as the moon moves west;
and as the moon sinks, the one
on the carpet stretches and
grows vaguer, and then less white,
smudging the shadow of chair

leg as of couch shoulder.
The one on the ceiling dims,
stretching, too. Is yellower.
And then the moon, orange again,
duskier, sinks to the earth,
goes down. It was time to go
to bed in the first place. Go.

Wanting More Than There Is

1
I thin myself to the surface of water,
transparent, reflecting
light, brushing air, keeping
at an even distance from the clouds
and from the crystal, pink, orange, white
pebbles, from the silt, crabs,
sliding starfish, a needle-fish fire-hosing
around a clump of mussels —
clear, faintest green,
a lens;
level, easy where I am, or
lifted by the tide, the same; or into waves.

2
The sun plunges west —
the dry, gray dock,
the green creek whirled by a boat's wash
into Queen Anne's lace;
two red-billed skimmers like swooping
fighters in the shadow of a marshy bank.
Gold-leaf, and then moon-foil,
a miraculous commotion,
stars.

3
At five o'clock, in the first gray light,
a wedge of tiny, fanning ripples
like a feather
wanders on the incoming tide: somebody
struggling. I cup him up, a
half-inch moth, white, gray, and tan
like marbling on an old book,
with delicate crimson antennae.

A Sunny, Winter Day

The birdbath is a dish of snow.
The lawn chairs keep the attitudes
of summer noons and starry nights.

I read. You might drive in the drive
and we might talk in the snowy chairs.
A sunny, winter day as flat as Kansas.

Girl in an Apartment Window

At my sink, I'm running
water for coffee.

A Degas lit in brick,
your window

shows you lifting your gown
over your head,

torso, breasts in the light.
You gather

it like a cloud, bend,
vanish, come

back buttoning a shirt,
tossing

hair outside the collar.
Then, other

windows become other poses.
In one you're

by a table, looking down,
cup in hand.

Everything Comes Eventually

As, today, May's shirtsleeve air,
dogs, jonquils, girls,
sunlit past seven o'clock; or

as, in time, the first snow rasping
brown oak leaves.
Love, too. And the end of it.

Hurricane

At eight that morning, blue light flashing,
a police car bullhorned the news:
the island was being evacuated.
We chose to stay. We sat with coffee
at the windows, watching the green marsh
fold and sway to the wind. Pounding
past the Outer Banks, she'd come all night
NNE, keeping off the coast,
eye steady, a locomotive's light,
her wild skirts whirling all before her.

        All morning cars
topped with bikes and beach umbrellas lined
the causeway road. I trimmed the hedge
and dumped the cut brush in the pines
and poison ivy. At noon we went
like kids along the gray sand
where breakers lashed the ocean milky
or, hulking under the inlet's glass,
hurled up among the bulkhead boulders
at our feet, bomb-gouts, feathers.

After the thronged and sunny days,
the shore, deserted, seemed like home;
shops shut, the field of tennis courts
black and rain-swept, sky fuming granite.
The radio said she was on course
and should pass just offshore — unless
willfully she turned to grind on shore.
We packed books, odds and ends, in case.
We fueled the lantern. We closed and locked,
stowed, bolted, shuttered, and tied down.

Rain peppered the picture window
obscuring the salt-creek, the marsh
beyond. Wind bulged it, bending the room,

lamp, us, the sandy, tangled sheets,
until we half-feared it might shatter
and explode. She was on course,
flinging at ninety miles an hour
mimosa fronds and rain —
August afternoon dark as November,
a swirling cauldron big as Texas.

Two hours till high, the driven tide
went on rising. On the dock we huddled
in sodden hoods as waves unrolled
all down the creek, sloshing up between
dock-boards, washing level, lifting
over them and running to our ankles.
Great wreaths and thatch of dry marsh grass
lifted on the flood, swirled, bobbed,
unbroken water stretching away.
The birds had disappeared — gulls, terns,
ospreys from their nests in the dead cedars.
Next door, a cruiser screaked and waddled
in its shortened ropes and yelping pulleys.
Rain like bullets whanged and slapped.
We moved the cars to higher ground,
shouting, leaning against hard wind.

        As if it were black paint,
the wet black roared and spattered, pressed
against the windows, till nothing outside
was visible. Walls shuddered. On TV
we watched the storm — in gray, frail
images of empty streets, wind, rain,
an electric line loose and threshing
over cars. Little clear runnels
squeezed between the panes and frames,
pooling on the sills.

                Outside,
the cedars by the house like waves
tossed in the wind. Streetlights rattled,

signs rattled, poles leaned like daisies.
Full dark at not quite five o'clock,
two feet of ocean in the road,
we pushed to where the ocean now
crashed over the causeway, heaving bricks
and old tires, chomping, sucking chunks
of asphalt from the road. A beer can
zinged into half-floating bayberry. Sand
stung like nettles.

Why had we stayed, why had we come?
Roar nailed us into selves, voiceless,
gesturing.

        Far down the creek,
flood-lit, three figures in yellow slickers
struggled with a swamping Whaler.
We went to help, past curbs and bushes
wading the thigh-deep swells and furrows
in the road, rain molten on our faces.
We shouted, jerked the jerking lines,
dodged gunwales thumping up on pilings,
until at last it steadied, rode.

Blackness was turning gray, and lights
began to show far up the creek,
in town. Like a dance of saws,
the water bucked and thrust, but the tide
had topped and then began to slide out,
twisting, bouncing seaward marsh-thatch,
boards, an oar, debris.

        So that was all.

A little light leaked in the west.
The wind had turned, behind her,
but she was pounding faithfully
on NNE — to smash at daybreak
against Long Island.

Goats in the Road

We were on our way probably
to Marvão, and as we came up
to the curve of the mountain road,
we came upon goats, belled,
chiming in the road. We stopped
and, I think, had a smoke and
looked out over the tan and green
of mid-summer Portugal. Thirty
or so, blocking the way, straggling
on the bluff. We waded them
like a sea.

       No one else
remembers, and you no longer want
to remember.

       And we drove on
to Marvão, that white, medieval-walled
town high on its crag
above the plains and the frontier,
fortified first by the Romans
— if it was that day —
and surely we made love
in the inn in the old convent,
but I remember only the balcony
and our watching together the far,
spidery lights of a village or two
and, across the border, the unbroken
blackness.

       Am I recalling
that day, or another time we came
to Marvão, or both? Which
of the thousand times we made love
stays in my mind?

            Oh, but the goats
happened once and once only.

                        Was it,
having quarreled, we did not make love
and I sat, after you were asleep,
smoking, looking out across
dark Spain?

            The map tells me nothing.
The Romans called their outpost here
Herminio Minor.

            Goats in the road,
though, silky brown, with bells —
and for a moment all of space,
wise with stars, blazed in the sunlight
of a summer day around us,
tinkling.

            Turn to your lover,
love, whether you have quarreled
or not, and hold him tight.
You can not hold him tight enough.
We drove on down that winding road
and left, like music in the air,
that music in the air.

The Girl Writing Her English Paper

lies on one hip by the fire,
blond, in jeans.

The wreckage of her labor, elegant as Eden
or petals from a tree,
surrounds her —

a little farm, smoke rising from the ashtray,
book, notebooks, papers, fields;
a poem's furrows.

If the lights were to go out suddenly,
stars would be overhead,
the edge of the woods dark and still.

Poetry

"Omissions are not accidents." — M.M.

It may be a thing
as the sea is, swaying,

huge, and featureless,
of which even pieces

piling and shoving
miss heaven —

have no beaks, no eyes,
or propensity to rise

except in turmoil.
Or it may be, though small,

a self: as a gull
makes a calm

drifting on the roughest
ocean, or as in a wave's trough

sandpipers mark out discipline
in lines

of flight. Why be modest?
It may be blessed

like the osprey with claws
it dares use.

Power that doesn't know what it's doing
isn't dominion;

nor is vastness all.
Initials

may seem a very pair of birds
thrusting heavenwards.

Myth, Commerce, and Coffee on United Flight #622 from Cleveland to Norfolk

Clouds, like bird-tracked snow,
spread to dawn-sun five miles below,

while businessmen (& poets) flow
on air streams, to and fro.

Now, of course, we know
Icarus could have made a go,

formed Attic Airways Co.,
expanded, advertised, and so

have carried Homer and Sappho
from Athens to Ilo

on reading tours — with, below,
clouds spread out like bird-tracked snow.

Chez T. S. Eliot

Too late to catch the last train home
    (a contretemps kind friends may spare us),
I sometimes spent the night at Tom's
    at 57 Chester Terrace.*

He and his first wife, Vivienne,
    were glad to put me up in, well, the
sitting room of their small house
    between Belgravia and Chelsea.

When after one such night I woke,
    I saw the hall door softly open
(it wasn't even seven o'clock)
    and fingers, then a hand grope in

to full arm's reach and from its hook
    in the dim light, still as a ghost,
lightly lift off a bowler hat
    and disappear. It was my host,

of course, who with a burglar's tread
    and manner circumspect and nervous
was setting off, prayer-book in hand,
    to go to early Sunday service.

The Author

for John Updike

O metamorphosis!
the poet's changing look
in jacket photographs
from slim book to slim book:

1) At twenty-five, thin, shy,
       having eaten the canary,
    he lounges outdoors in
       a black canvas sling chair

    he let the photographer
       and his young wife drag out
    from living room to lawn,
       and carefully move about

    till the New England eagle —
       its gilt wings spread for flight
    on the garage — would show
       (unfocussed, upper right).

    His rumpled sweater, a string
       from one turned sleeve, attest
    that summer's gone and that
       he's rather unimpressed,

    as does, in fingers curled,
       the thoughtful cigaret.
    A rose or two, limp iris,
       bespeak a mild regret.

    The picture's edge trims off
       his legs above the knee;
    the slacks are flannel, creased,
       and of good quality.

The future all before him,
    keen, casual, sits the bard
in not quite full profile,
    young, in a rented garden.

He awaits the shutter's click —
    cut fifties-close his locks,
his eyes fixed on the distant
    (perhaps some hollyhocks).

2)   At thirty, now, five summers
    having passed meanwhile,
he stands before a beach,
    tousled, Kennedy-style.

The sky a blur, it is
    a hazy, dampish day.
Behind his head, the sea's
    a band of flat, pale gray.

Raffish, off-hand, his hands
    behind his back (one's in
the chinos' left hip pocket),
    he squints a toothy grin.

Only his torso shows,
    but an inch of leg implies
one foot in conqueror's pose,
    on something piling-size.

Smokes in pocket, his shirt
    is striped and button-down
but tieless, loose, sleeves rolled:
    he prospers up in town.

Kids huddle at some game
    on the high sand, past one shoulder;
and past the other, lies
    a row of girls who're older.

Nobody's in the surf.
    As if looking for a ship
one moppet (upper right)
    stands puzzled at sea's lip.

His own kids are at home.
    He didn't come to swim.
The crinkles at his eyes
    suggest it's fun being him.

3)   Midpoint, in '69,
    the poet's thirty-six:
close-up, full face, hair mussed
    in the carefullest of the pics.

The edge cuts off left arm,
    right elbow, jacket button.
In back, a venetian blind
    conceals what it's shut on.

Appropriate for Nixon's
    first year, if nothing else,
tailored and crisp, his suit
    has executive lapels,

which frame a narrow tie
    with little flowery dots,
but it is twisted, showing
    he doesn't like it lots.

He sits, crinkles in jacket,
    right shoulder tilted down,
and leans the (unseen) elbow
    upon a something (not shown)

and partly fanned-up fingers
    hold glasses by one stem
while he sucks thoughtfully
    on the other hook of them.

The resulting pout draws down
    his fuller chin and cheeks;
his eyebrows arch up toward
    a somehow worried peak.

Droll, sad, he looks above
    the camera's level height
and in his pupils glows
    the flash's baleful light.

4) Eight years — kids growing up,
        divorce, books coming slower —
    he idles, hands in pockets,
        by a closed garage door

    set in a rustic façade
        of shingled barn (he did
    the shingling all himself),
        an exurban height and width

    that dwarf him, head to toe,
        dwindled to less than half
    the vertical display
        of this spacious photograph.

He's wearing rumpled chinos,
  knee-pointy (what the heck),
two sweaters, a light one
  over a dark turtleneck.

He has a little pot;
  his hair, a little gray.
He stands in crunchy leaves
  that cover the driveway

and wash against the bottom
  of the weathered wall as though
the clumps of dry grass there
  were sea-spray frozen so.

Shiny, well-kept, a window's
  lower panes (at crop,
far upper left) reflect
  a bare tree's twiggy top.

He neither smiles nor frowns,
  is neither pleased nor un-.
The old gunfighter awaits
  the cameraman, his son.

The Basement: 1937

The furnace has wild hair of pipes,
    fire glows within its door;
the coalbin, dark and massy, glints
    in bulblight from the stair.

Jars, lead-lidded beets, green beans,
    wax-topped strawberry jam,
squat on the dim shelves of the little
    slat-doored, spidered room.

Along one wall, on a wooden stand,
    the dead grandmother's trunk
keeps cool and flat her spectacles,
    the letters, laces, silks.

No one else seems frightened that
    this is under the whole house.
A peaceful look startles on even
    the dead faces of the mice.

Ice Cream

My father on a campstool
in the doorway of the white garage

cranks the old slat-and-wire freezer,
one hand holding down

the iron dome. Rock salt and ice
crunch round and round.

A Sunday, in the shade,
in July of '45,

war nearly over. Behind,
in the dirt-floored, bare-raftered

garage is hidden a half-pint
of Old Grand Dad

in a paper bag. The sun is hot
along the alley, on hollyhocks;

by the tap, the mint is dusty.
He turns the stiffening handle, not looking up.

The handle is like a long bead.
It turns upon a metal stem.

The Gold Nest

My father's father gave
this pocket watch to him
the summer he was ten.

He wore its slender gold
in darkness at his belly,
laid it by his bed.

It ticked for forty years,
and has for forty more
been silent, in a drawer.

One twist of the ribbed knob
would set its nest of tiny
spiders crawling again.

Kick the Can

In the still after-suppers of summer
kids playing kick-the-can, like small
ghosts flicking here and there among
the trees, across the lawns, hold off

the weight of darkness. And the lights
go on in houses: radios tell
the weather, Doolittle over Tokyo,
or Robert Kennedy in L. A.

Hidden too well, deep in the barberry
by widower McCann's white porch,
or in the tomato patches in yards
beyond the unlit alley, I hear

the can go clunking down the walk
and "One-two-three" and "All-in-free."
The years go by. I am not caught,
nor called home, all the long dark long.

For a Long Time

You were not born. I saw from a train window
in a foreign city, in early dark,
in fallen snow, in streetlight,
a bus queue at the top of the rise
where the road came up from the underpass.
A few flakes fell like petals.

I can not guess what city.

        And I saw
a car's white lights turning into a black
suburban street, snowy, where I would never go.

In Highgate Cemetery

I had not counted on this patchwork
of the dead, crazy-quilt in vines,
brambles, weeds; the mausoleums
with broken windows, and every stone
tilted or toppled, the graves ramshackle,
crowded, the slabs of worn stone rotted,
slid, sunken, lurching, as if at sea.
In thin December sun, the yews.
The main path, muddy but half-tended,
leads round to where, on its giant marble,
huge, bearded, blackened, Marx's head
in bronze stares eyeless out across
the scuttled graves. A few cut flowers,
drooping, but bright and papery.
"Philosophy interprets the world . . .
The point, however, is to change it."

A row of newish Council flats
overlooks this hundred years of death,
overgrown and sliding down the hillside,
ghastly enough for a horror movie,
obelisks, chipped angels, marble scrolls,
the unkept promises of memory.
Among good burghers and baronets
George Eliot lies here, Rossetti's
red-haired Elizabeth (whom he
exhumed after eight years for poems
buried by her cheek), Pound's Fenellosa,
and, more recently, the poor —
new stones with Polish names, here, there,
or, older, wooden crosses rotting
at the base, hand-lettered names —
a final, helpless ragtag, for cash,
before the place is closed, the gate

sealed up, where all these dead have risen
again in saplings, berries, ivy
that climbs the standing crosses and lifts
arms outspread like fluttering Druids.
Two keepers chop and pile and burn
the undergrowth, and so to heaven.
Death's not so scary. All of London
lies in view, oil storage drums,
skyscrapers, steeples, smoky Thames.

Footnote

The aviation fuel that drove
the humming engines of the JU-88's
above Madrid, stringing down the bombs,
was made here in the States: by Texaco.

The Monday-Banner

It   is dollar-green & so long
it   takes nearly everybody to hold
it   over their heads and march along under
it.

We

Oh, we would die here, in the snow,
if the gas companies and oil sheiks
chose. If the trucks didn't come,
if somebody didn't want our money,
if the vast fluorescent stores
emptied and shut down. Some might
walk out, but most of us would crouch
in houses, burning sticks of them
for a little warmth, in the non-electric
dark; finding weapons, if no one
came for us. We could not survive
like the few, first settlers in the woods.
Perhaps we should die on the road,
in the snow, the burning cities behind us.

F-14's Practicing
for the Weekend Air Show

Six jets, a tight triangle,
    themselves triangular,
knife the cool August blue.
    I see them — from my car

light-stopped in the rush hour
    by churches in storefronts,
wire-windowed delis, rib
    joints — veer as one to, roaring,

vanish. Red turns green.
    And swiftly we also,
homeward, air-conditioned,
    in close formation go.

The Fear

Our old dog's frightened of the wind.
When a front moves through, she senses
the pressure before the sky darkens
or the air stirs. Firecrackers wake her.
She cowers on backporch or crawls
under the kitchen table, inconsolable.
At night she sleeps more and more
under the bed — and that's not enough
when the curtains billow and streetlight
floods the sill. Nothing assures her.
No touch comforts the quaking in her soul
at far-off fireworks or rolls of thunder,
or the hush of dawn rain. I wake
to her watchful silhouette.
I leave my hand on her back, but she
listens, stiff, and shudders a little
from time to time. So we get up
at least, to wait for the morning paper
and for sunrise, or for whatever it is
in snow or rain she knows is there.

Riding in a Stranger's Funeral

It is now 24 years since I rode in a stranger's funeral,
waved into the procession, at a stop light,
by a policeman who mistook my having my headlights on
in the daylight (to spare an overcharging battery).

Then I saw the cars behind with lights on, too,
and little pennants on their fenders,
and I understood. That was in blossomy April
in Lynchburg, and I did not turn off or drop aside

because I feared the cars behind might follow me.
So I went on, trees, shops, dogs, and passersby
on the sidewalks alongside, going about their affairs,
sunshine through the windshield warm on my knees.

And I said to myself that any man justly
might mourn any other, since none can live forever,
and that someday, too, who knew when,
I might ride similarly surprised, but in the lead.

At the natural-stone gateway when, instead of turning,
I drove straight on, my kitetail of cars correctly
turned and followed the other cars following the hearse,
into the cemetery, and in among the trees.

When You Buy a Big, Old House

You get the straight-grain oak (cut in 1910, seeded in 1850)
and the soft and clogged pipes, wiring with rotting insulation,
plaster whose patches, like big white balloons flattened
to the basement ceilings, recall excitement and long to fall.

Some things you fix, and the place is bright and comfortable
in the morning sunlight of new Junes, snug in up-to-date snows
and winds that go on looking for cracks under the eaves —
the old ark creaks, but its fireplace flutters with cheery warmth;

and you realize it's more to you than you are to it.
Patient of ruin, the beams and struts will go on sheltering you
as long as you need or care. Like a cave, it has its secrets.
Somebody probably died in it, or you fall to imagining

a little girl whose bedroom you have made your study,
who grew up there and slept and dreamed of gifts and lovers,
and might be young still or, from earlier, a grandmother in Phoenix.
Who knows? Old plays that ran, and closed, and are forgotten.

Such made-up, sentimental ghosts don't haunt anybody.
Just call the plumber and get on with your own life.
Enough that, at the dark bottom of its well, in the gray silt,
a sash-weight leans, remembering.

Tell the Chipmunk

You're up at six. The summer
    light's under way
and a high branch of the cherry,
    you notice, holds
like paper bells, in a row,
    a twig of leaves
brown amid the flourishing.
    Some signal tells
the tree: make a stick.
    There waits, on the edge
of the driveway, this pile
    a whole hawthorn
became last year, chunks, logs
    still drying toward
next winter's fire. It makes
    a handy house,
this year, for some chipmunks —
    of whom this one,
now also up at six,
    comes toddling tail-
up back across the driveway
    from somewhere, sits
on the pile and takes in
    whatever a
chipmunk takes in of this,
    the common summer.
If you didn't have a use
    for firewood, you'd
tell him or her, Relax,
    enjoy; whatever
this is we're all into,
    we're all in it
together, & so forth.
    Tell the chipmunk
about fear, then, or somebody's
    not loving you!

Thinking about Gravesites

The vet said your leaky ticker might not last
the weekend, but it did. And here we are
on the back steps, having this idle time,
a cool, blue, sunny August evening
after clinic, X-ray, EKG, shots, pills.

There isn't much we can do, sit side by side
on the shady steps, regretting nothing.
No chasing a tennis ball bounced off the garage.
No walk. At bedtime I'll carry you up
the stairs, but now this moment out of time.

We may, who knows, be thinking the same scenes.
If I say *Maggie swim,* would you see again
the gulls, the dock, the swift Atlantic creek
of half your summers? or *Honeybear,* recall
that long-dead pal? Memory is painful.

A cardinal threads the pin oak and cherry,
stitching an evening that's too fine to lose.
But of course we do lose everything,
and even practice a little every day:
we go away, come back, and go away.

Your favorite hiding place from thunder-booms
was under the viburnum we had to chop out
and replace with this stick of greenspire linden
and pachysandra, but that will be your place.
You'll never miss a summer evening here.

The rest of us will get dragged off and stuck
in some strange hole, but you'll be here.
Stay. Hold the fork. We won't, at last, be back.

The Poem

The impulse takes its form,
    the seed remembers:
a trash of portulaca
    and of marigolds
(say) becoming, being
    again. These bushes
of little suns, oh these
    sprawling, reaching
little roses! A crack
    in the asphalt edge
of the driveway, good as any.
    My neighbor's daisies
slide downhill, past the fence;
    stand up. All this
is going on all winter,
    secret and hidden
as it snows, in the snow-melt.
    Of course. The fields
and woods aren't buying seeds
    in little packets.
Why praise a hybrid's mauve
    originality?
All this was handled well
    enough, before
we somehow came upon
    the dull illusion
that the carefullest garden
    also isn't wild.

After a Time

After a time you don't recall
the row you sat in in third grade,
bedroom curtains your first wife made.

Things that were important fade.
Who was to blame? Were you afraid?
The past becomes a story.

It was, you think, not that at all.
You remember, brown, red, a tie,
but not the color of an eye.

Now in the telling, what's a lie?
The bluff you leapt from was how high?
Fact grows illusory.

Things that were important fade.
Now in the telling, what's a lie?
After a time you don't recall.
The past becomes a story.

NOTES

The section epigraph on p. [11] is from conversation quoted in
James Lord, *A Giacometti Portrait,* The Museum of Modern Art;
that on p. [47], from "Credences of Summer," 11. 31–32, in
The Collected Poems of Wallace Stevens.

The creatures of "The Dictionary Zoo," pp. 23–25, may be
found in *The American College Dictionary.*

In "A Last Photograph," p. 32, 1. 10 assumes the original
(unhappy) ending to Dickens' *Great Expectations.*

"What He Says," p. 34. The figure is drawn from William Carlos
Williams, in Rutherford, 1960.

"Ungainly Things," pp. 38–39, is based on an account in *A
Bestiary by Toulouse-Lautrec,* The Fogg Art Museum and The
Harvard College Library, 1954.

"Fable," p. 40. Cf. Richard Poirier, in *The Renewal of Literature,*
1987: "If Shakespeare had never existed we would not miss his
works, for there would be nothing missing."

"Poetry," p. 85. The epigraph (with initials) is the entire
"Author's Note" at the front of *The Complete Poems of Marianne
Moore,* 1967. She was doubtless referring to the astonishing
revision of her famous "Poetry," a poem she had struggled with
at least since its first publication in 1921.

"Chez T. S. Eliot," p. 87. After Sir Herbert Read, quoted in
James Sutherland, *The Oxford Book of Literary Ancedotes,* 1975.

> * This Chester Terrace, in 1983,
> is not the one in *London A to Z;*
> that's somewhere up by Regent's Park. Turns out,
> as the folks next door at 55 recount,
> the name changed more than thirty years ago:
> so Chester Terrace is now Chester Row.
> The Tube's Victoria, whence a short walk
> a little west will let you come to gawk.

"The Author," pp. 88–92, describes the dustjacket photographs of John Updike's first four books of poems.

"Kick the Can," p. 96. General Jimmy Doolittle's bombing of Tokyo occurred on 18 April (1942) rather than in June or so the poem suggests. My nine-year-old's impression has obviously switched that raid with the battle of Midway.

"Thinking about Gravesites," p. 107. "Hold the fork" is a whimsical variation of "Hold the fort." In talking to dogs, the general sound of the phrases they know matters, not exact words, so language has a continuing, amusing elasticity human speech seldom enjoys.

Thanks to Bruce Bennett, Mark Irwin, and especially Peter Klappert for suggestions about this MS. Where I have persevered in folly, they are not to blame.

A number of poems in the second section were written during the period of a fellowship granted by the National Endowment for the Arts.